HOW TO

MANAGE MONEY

WHAT THEY DON'T TEACH US IN SCHOOL

ZACH TURNER

HOW TO

MANAGE MONEY

WHAT THEY DON'T TEACH US IN SCHOOL

ZACH TURNER

CONTENTS

INTRODUCTION

DISCLAIMER

Before reading this book, please make sure you understand the following: This is not financial advice; it is simply informational and personal opinions with hopes to educate and not give advice. The content is intended to be used, and must be used, for informational purposes only. Make sure to do your own analysis and research before making any investment based on your own personal circumstances. You should take independent financial advice from a professional/ chartered financial advisor (see end of book for more info).

This is **not** a 'get rich quick' scheme, this is **not** a guide to forex trading, this is **not** some kind of 'pyramid' scheme.

This eBook was written purely to give a basic understanding of the fundamentals to personal finance. It is aimed at those who are wanting to start their journey to financial freedom, to step onto the correct pathway to becoming debt-free and to begin raising their capital.

I do not intend this handbook to be at all confusing to the average individual who does not have a background in financing.

Personal finance is a subject that the majority of us are not taught in school; some may go onto study it at college and/or university. But for most of us, we come out of education wondering where our money is and why we are struggling from paycheck to paycheck.

In a controversial sense, our national education curriculum is not there to create successful, wealthy, financial advocates. Education is just there to teach you the basics of how to be an employee in certain subjects and fields.

However, on a more positive note, you do not need to time travel back to the beginning of your life and start again. It does not matter how old you are or how young you are; you can simply start to learn the basics of finance today and watch your wealth begin to grow alongside your knowledge.

This is why I am writing this handbook today, to develop your thought process and positively change your view on money. You will learn how cash can work for you and how monthly bills or taxes are not the issue.

Everything stated may or may not fit into your lifestyle or your future goals. This is not advice but more of a loose guideline or perhaps an eye-opener to new foundations. Ensure you perform your own research into everything.

HOW TO SAVE EMERGENCY FUNDS (SAVINGS)

The first subject on my list of things to discuss is my ideology on the word "savings". This will involve some ideas that you may not agree with, but I want you to open your mind and see for yourself why most financial advisors, some famous investors and successful business persons all have similar mindsets when it comes to saving money in the form of cash (free funds within your bank account).

Firstly, before you start worrying about your future emergency debts, you need to pay off your current debts, as this will be cheaper in the long run if you focus on paying these off now. The reason why current debts need to be paid off as soon as possible is because as months pass by, you are paying unnecessary interest rates on your loans, which inevitably digs a deeper financial hole.

This applies to you if you have:

- Credit card debt
- Unarranged overdraft/s
- Personal loans or pay-day loans
- Arrears on your mortgage payments

Do You Want Your Money To Grow Or To Shrink?

This is a question with a very obvious answer: **GROW!**

Unfortunately, the steps that achieve the answer are not so obvious. From a young age, everybody has been taught that putting money away inside a savings account is the best way for anybody to be able to afford the things they want in the future. However, as time goes by and years go on, banks are increasingly paying people **less and less** for saving money within their accounts. To get a better understanding of how to make money grow **more and more,** we need to understand the importance of interest rates and why they are no longer the core to producing money.

Let's start by taking a look at the **1980s,** when banks began the decade by paying their customers an average of **10.50% annual interest** on their savings. This means if the bank's customer held £1000 within their savings account at the start of 1980, by 1981 their £1000 would be worth £1105. Sure, at first this may not sound like a substantial amount of growth to you, but this is actually incredible for such a "risk free" way of saving money. Why did I just put that into quotation marks? Let me explain…

Although your money will not (yet) be at risk of decreasing whilst sitting inside a savings account, it is at risk of **not increasingly growing**.

Let's compare those 1980s figures to 2021:

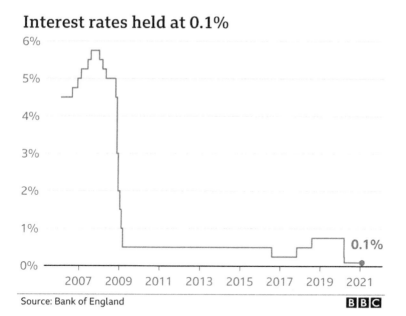

Interest rates held at 0.1%

Source: Bank of England

BBC

As displayed in the graph, from 2008 to 2021, the Bank of England base rate fell to as low as 0.1%. This base rate determines how much interest the Bank of England pays to the institutions that hold money with them, meaning the lower they pay out to the institutions using it, the lower the institutions pay out to their customers for using them. We are now seeing an average of **0.64% annual interest** on savings accounts in the UK.

So let's refer to that £1000 that returned to us a **hefty** £105 after a year in 1980. If we were to save £1000 today, by next year, it would have returned us £6.40! That's almost twenty-five Freddos! As you can see nowadays, if you want your money to grow itself, then a savings account may not be the best option. In fact, it is predicted that the UK will soon be seeing **negative interest** rates. Although this more than likely will not affect the average saver, it is still possible.

Inflation

The fact that you are getting paid less to save may seem like a bad thing, but it generally is not. Inflation and interest rates are intrinsically linked. When the inflation rates are high, interest rates go up alongside; therefore, you earn more money on your savings, but in return, the cost of basic goods is higher and the cost of financially borrowing is also at an increased value.

So Are You Saying That I Should Not Save Money In A Savings Account?

No. Savings are still important to everybody, even big companies. Just keep in mind that a savings account should probably **not** be the main haven for your incoming cash if you are wanting to grow your wealth. Finding the right balance for each individual's budget can really help to accelerate financial growth. I recommend speaking to a financial advisor with the goals that you have in mind and asking them to put together a plan for your money.

Everybody has different circumstances, goals and priorities, which is why it is important to speak to a financial advisor to ensure that you are on the right path for what **you** want to achieve. Below is an **example** of a very basic plan:

Put aside 25% (more if you don't have many commitments) from your monthly wage into a savings account every single month until you have reached around £2000-£5000, depending on the amount of things that could go wrong in your life, for example, vet bills, vehicle breakdown, property failures or job loss. We will call this the 'emergency fund'.

In my honest opinion, if you do **NOT** have at least £2000 saved right now, you should **NOT** be eating at fancy restaurants, looking to upgrade your working phone or perfectly functioning car and you certainly should **NOT** be scrolling designer fashion websites to buy your next Gucci handbag. This is all something that should be classed as a treat once earning the right to do so. Do not fall into the consumerism trap.

Once you have saved your emergency fund, you can start to loosen up a little bit, and by this I only mean a little bit and no more. This is because the next step is to continue putting aside monthly income. However, this time, you should consider **reducing** your monthly savings to 10% and instead **investing** the remaining 15% of your monthly income.

An ideal target for a total savings account is for it to be the same amount as three to six months' worth of monthly outgoings. As an example, if you pay £1000 a month on necessary expenses such as food, rent, and insurance, then it is advised to have £3000-£6000 within your savings account in case you were to lose your job or your investments were to temporarily crash or emergencies suddenly happened such as home repairs, vet bills, and car failures.

This is known as free cash, or in our case, **emergency funds**.

HOW TO CLEAR DEBT

If you are in debt, please do not think that you are alone. The average UK adult is £30,575 in debt, according to the Bank of England (which does not include student loans in that figure). There is also plenty of support and guidance that can be found online, a lot of the time for free!

When a person is in debt, their salary is simply in a rat race versus their debt. Each month the employer may as well just directly pay the employee's bank or whichever institute is loaning them the money. Nobody wants to work hard to pay somebody else, but unfortunately, this is the reality of borrowing.

> *"I'm going to enjoy every second, and I'm going*
> *to know I'm enjoying it while I'm enjoying it.*
> *Most people don't live; they just race. They*
> *are trying to reach some goal far away on the*
> *horizon, and in the heat of the going they get so*

*breathless and panting that they lose sight of
the beautiful, tranquil country they are passing
through; and then the first thing they know,
they are old and worn out, and it doesn't make
any difference whether they've reached the goal
or not." - Jean Webster*

People are raised to believe that the higher somebody's salary is, the less likely that person is going to be in debt, but this is proven to be false. In fact, what happens when somebody is not financially smart is simple:

**The more they earn, the more expensive
their liabilities/expenses become.**

Refinancing

Refinancing your mortgage or your car may come across as a wise idea for paying off your debts (especially when the bank is trying their hardest to **sell** the idea to you); unfortunately, this is not always the case. Monthly payments may become lower and appear more attractive, but the borrower will eventually end up paying a greater total amount than before. When refinancing a loan, the bank will either want the borrower to take out more money than necessary or to extend their loan. Let's look at an extreme example to explain why this is probably not the best choice for clearing debt.

£500,000 Mortgage @ 5% Interest	£2,700/month
10 years pass by (you have 20 years left on mortgage)	
£400,000 left @ 3% Interest	£2,400/month
£550,000 refinance + 30 Years extension	

Yes, refinancing means that the borrower is paying smaller payments monthly. However, it also means that they will be paying these monthly payments forever. Instead, what you should do is continue paying your original monthly amount with no interest added.

So what should I do to pay off my debts?

As I have mentioned, there is plenty of support online. Financial advisors can also help but usually for a fee. For now, just try to build a good financial habit and keep working towards those goals.

Simply put: **earn more, spend less, save and invest**. It's not as easy as it sounds though. It is all down to you mentally training yourself to do this. Just remember it's only a temporary sacrifice until you are debt-free!

Here are a few examples of what you can do to ensure you're spending less:

- Cook/prepare your own food whether it's for lunches at work or dinners at home.

- Stop unnecessarily buying food/drink when you can stick to the basics.

- Stop buying expensive clothing when cheap clothes can look just as good on you.

- Do not use any more credit. If you can't afford it, don't buy it.

Once you have trained yourself to spend less, it's time to earn more. But do **NOT** ever go back to your old **bad habits**.

- Work harder and get a pay raise at work.

- Make yourself more valuable to companies and yourself by learning new skills.

- Freelance side hustles such as writing music/ creating music/writing books/photography where you can sell your creativity.

HOW TO MAKE MONEY LAST

Making money last longer is an incredibly important tool for being able to pay off liabilities. This can be achieved by setting rules or budgets for how to spend money. For example, I personally use the rule "If you **want** something but **can't** afford to buy it ten times, find a cheaper alternative or don't buy it at all." This rule helps me to make my money last.

Think about it, if you only had £100 in £10 notes and you accidentally were to drop £10, it would be gutting, but it wouldn't be the worst. However, if you dropped £60 of that £100, you would be stressed when you could not find the money. So why would you spend 60% of your worth on an item that depreciates in value from the minute it's bought?

One answer: **the consumerism mindset.**

"All over the place, from the popular culture to the propaganda system, there is constant pressure to make people feel that they are helpless, that the only role they can have is to ratify decisions and to consume." - Noam Chomsky

One of the biggest key factors to remember is that **the mind is the most powerful tool** that anybody can possess. It can either be neglected and untrained, or the mind can be trained in such a way that it starts to view money from a whole different perspective. Training the mind to **turn away from excessive consumerism** and stepping into a minimalistic frame of mind is an alternative approach to becoming financially free.

"Wanting less is a better blessing than having more." - Mary Ellen Edmunds

There are many simple ways that we can process our thoughts to produce a better outcome. We can ask, "Why should I buy this **liability** that is going to **depreciate** in value? I can put the exact same amount of money into an **asset** that will **appreciate** in value!" To see more about the comparison between assets and liabilities, skip ahead to 'How To Balance Money'.

BUDGETING!

A crucial approach to making money last from paycheck to paycheck is to use a budgeting spreadsheet to track incoming/outgoing payments. This will detail how much money is left over once you have deducted bills from your monthly income, allowing you to budget your spending money on weekly shopping. Here's an example:

Expenses				Income			
Date	Amount	Description	Category	Date	Amount	Description	Category
15/03/2021	£50.00	Car Insurance	Car	01/03/2021	£1,700.00	Salary	Paycheck
20/03/2021	£10.00	Phone Bill	Utilities				
25/03/2021	£500.00	Mortgage	Home				
01/03/2021	£300.00	Credit Card	Utilities				
01/03/2021	£250.00	Car Finance	Car				

Increase in total savings
£590.00
Saved this month

	START BALANCE	END BALANCE
	£0.00	£590.00

Expenses

Planned	£0.00
Actual	£1,110.00

Income

Planned	£0.00
Actual	£1,700.00

Expenses

	Planned	Actual	Diff.
Totals	£0.00	£1,110.00	-£1,110.00
Food/Drink	£0.00	£0.00	£0.00
Gifts	£0.00	£0.00	£0.00
Health/medical	£0.00	£0.00	£0.00
Home	£0.00	£500.00	-£500.00
Car	£0.00	£300.00	£300.00
Personal	£0.00	£0.00	£0.00
Music	£0.00	£0.00	£0.00
Utilities	£0.00	£310.00	-£310.00
Travel	£0.00	£0.00	£0.00
Overdraft Interest	£0.00	£0.00	£0.00
Movers		£0.00	£0.00

Income

	Planned	Actual	Diff.
Totals	£0.00	£1,700.00	£1,700.00
Savings	£0.00	£0.00	£0.00
Paycheck	£0.00	£1,700.00	£1,700.00
Bookles/Exchange	£0.00	£0.00	£0.00
Interest	£0.00	£0.00	£0.00
Other	£0.00	£0.00	£0.00
Movers	£0.00	£0.00	£0.00

As you can see, in this example budgeting spreadsheet, I am left with £590 after paying all my monthly bills. I then put 10% of my salary aside into a savings account (£170), leaving me with £420. This is £105 a week for grocery shopping/commuting expenses, which is more than enough.

Another key note to making money go further, that is often overlooked by most consumers, is whether or not you are paying too much for your bills. Once in a contract, over time, you get into a routine and adapt to paying this amount of money. Here are some guidelines to monthly direct debits:

- Try to avoid contracts where possible, as this way you can adapt to circumstantial changes.

- You should aim to make sure you are paying the right price for your consumption.

For example, if you're paying £40/month for your phone bill but only use 2GB of mobile data, you can easily cut back to just around £10/month. This will save you £30/month, which can be put towards a week's worth of shopping, credit card payments, investments or wherever it needs to go!

Of course something else to remember is the idea of cutting out monthly subscriptions that you do not need, such as streaming services. This can be an easy and quick solution to saving lots of money each month. Four £10 subscriptions is £40, which can be used elsewhere.

HOW TO BALANCE MONEY

Balancing, which can be physically displayed as a 'balance sheet', is a staple part of everybody's finances. Whether it is a successful multi-billion business or a student with a few thousand dollars, a healthily balance sheet is important to everybody.

Before understanding the ins and outs of a healthy or unhealthy balance sheet, you must first understand the importance of the difference between **assets and liabilities**.

Personal Assets

Generally speaking, an asset is anything that either holds or gains value and/or can be converted back into cash after it has been purchased. An asset is not something that loses value as soon as it is bought. In my opinion, it is best to view assets as something that is likely to generate a stream of income or returns.

Examples of personal assets that **gain value** would be the following:

- Investment properties (rent money, auction flips, DIY flips)

- Investment cars (not the average car, ones that are not to be driven)

- Artwork (a painting of Christ believed to be painted by DaVinci sold for $450 million; the very same painting sold at an auction 60 years ago for £45)

- Expensive wines/whiskies (as long as they're not drunk!)

- Valuable metals (gold, silver, platinum, etc.)

- Stocks, shares and bonds

Notice how I define properties and cars; these do not include your personal property/s or car/s. Some people class personal homes and cars as assets because they can be liquidated into cash. However, in my case, I do not consider them as assets; I consider them as liabilities. Your property **may** gain value over time, but it may already be valued at its utmost best. Meaning the money that you put into your home on repairs, design and family perfections could actually lose you money in the grand scheme of things. By the time it comes around to you deciding to sell up and move on, the house might have actually lost value. However, we will cover real estate more in depth later on under the 'How To Invest Your Money' section.

Personal Liabilities

By now, you have probably already guessed it: **liabilities are the opposite to assets.** Liabilities are payments that a person owes, usually in the form of money and items that depreciate in value.

Examples of liabilities:

- Personal loans/credit card
- Car finance
- Mortgage

Finding Your Balance

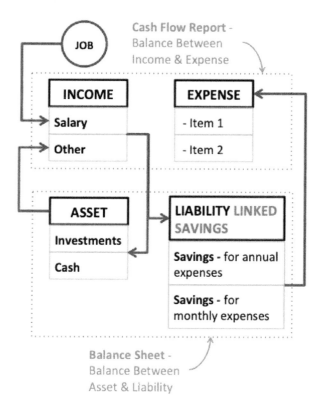

- Starting from the very top, these are your income and expense columns.

- You then take your income and convert it into assets, cash/investments.

- Your assets start generating more income, falling back into the income column.

- Which then partially goes back into your asset column (sounds like a money generator, right?).

- The money that has now been made from your assets alongside your salary can go into paying your liabilities and savings.

The perfect balance sheet will always show more assets than liabilities. Let's look at a very basic balance sheet to get a rough idea. You can always translate this into your own. It is important to understand that the term **current** defines assets or liabilities that are owed/owned within the current fiscal year.

CURRENT ASSETS

Rental Income	£11,760
Cash	£2000
Stocks & Shares	£5549
Other	£884
Total Current Assets	**£20,194**

CURRENT LIABILITIES

Mortgages	£12,550
Credit Card	£4000
Car Finance	£3450
Total Current Liabilities	**£20,000**
Equity (Net Worth)	**£194**

This is a positively balanced sheet because the assets outweigh the liabilities, meaning that job income is free to go into the asset column and to expand it even further.

As you can imagine, a negatively balanced sheet would display liabilities outweighing the assets, showing that year-over-year equity will be decreasing in value rather than increasing unless rebalanced.

You can easily create a table similar to this, listing all your assets and liabilities to get a better understanding of your financial position.

WHAT TO TAKE AWAY FROM THIS:

The importance of balancing your money is simple: If you want to **lose money,** then **buy liabilities,** but if you want to **grow your wealth,** simply spend your life **buying assets**. Use your assets to buy the luxuries, and do not use your liabilities to buy the luxuries.

HOW TO INVEST MONEY

ALL investing comes with a risk, so be sure to seek financial advice before investing. Perform plenty of research and due diligence. There are plenty of different areas to invest money in. Let's explore them.

- Which sector/s of investing do you prefer?
- How much risk are you willing to take, and how much risk do you need to take?
- Does the investment fit into your desired portfolio?

Firstly and most importantly, before investing into any asset, you must understand the risks that investors are exposed to.

(RISK MANAGEMENT AND RISK TOLERANCE)

An investor will be **exposed to a list of risks,** and it is best to go into investing with a plan and understanding of how to minimise exposure to these risks. This is known as 'risk management'.

An investor might want to **maximise returns** by exposing themselves to **larger risks** in order to potentially return **higher percentages**. **Bigger risk** means **higher volatility,** which results in much larger swings (portfolio moving up and down in great numbers as opposed to small dips/gains). This is known as 'risk tolerance'.

Many beginner investors who do not have a lot of capital to begin with invest directly into very high-risk stocks because they want to discover the next 500%/month returns. This of course is shadowed by a lot of risk. Although it can be possible to find a +500% return, it is also more than possible to see -90% returns, and if you're investing on margin, it can go even worse. Is this risk necessary?

As an example of what investors can expect to see, let's take a look at six different types of risk that investors are exposed to.

Price Risk

Price volatility is generally seen as the first/major risk when it comes to investing in any type of asset. Will the price go up?

Will the price go down? In the long term, equity prices statistically go up; however, to get there, the stock price will have a bumpy ride. This is known as volatility. Let's take a look at two graphs, one being the volatility index (the higher the VIX index, the higher the stock market volatility), and the other being the S&P 500 (top 500 US equity stocks), and let's compare the two to visualise how volatility affects the market.

When the volatility index goes up, the S&P 500 price comes down. This is because volatility generally happens during times of fear, as you can see by the small crash in March 2020 when the pandemic began shutting countries down. However, high volatility does not always mean dips in the market, as we can see at the start of 2018. This is because volatility can also resemble unusually large amounts of over-buying, but it is likely that the market will go through a correction after this happens.

To determine a stock's volatility is quite easy. Just take a look at the daily movement for the past few months.

The **less movement** => the **less volatility** => the **less risk** => the **less short-term returns** => the more **consistency.**

Risk is easily manageable; however, it can never be fully removed from the equation. Let's take a look at how we can achieve managed risk.

Equity vs Bonds

4,019.87

+46.98 (1.18%) ↑

1 Apr. 17 15 GMT-4 Disclaimer

INDEXSP: .INX

+ Follow

| 1 day | 5 days | 1 month | 6 months | YTD | 1 year | 5 years | Max |

| Open | 3,992.78 | High | 4,020.63 | Low | 3,992.78 |

If you are wanting to invest into highly-volatile equities, you can invest into something known as 'bonds' to balance out the amount of risk you are willing to take on. Bonds are an interest payment paid by government or corporate bodies. They borrow your money and pay you an interest rate depending on whether it's short-term or long-term and the current interest rates.

We typically see bonds as a much lower risk; this is because they are usually backed by the government. I'd suggest investing into government bonds rather than corporate ones. We all know the infamous story of Thomas Cook going under. Unfortunately, Thomas Cook also owed many people bond money, so those who had invested into TC bonds took a hard hit when they were subject to company liquidation.

A one-hundred percent equity portfolio is an extremely high-risk portfolio. You are subject to not being able to access your full investment money in times of market despair; if the stock market crashes, so does the entirety of your portfolio. If you're unable to stomach the 12%-50% crashes, or if you know that you will need the money within the upcoming few years, then this is not the right strategy for you. Typically, the average price move for the S&P 500 is 14.3%.

However, a one-hundred percent bond portfolio is an extremely low risk portfolio, quite the polar opposite to an equity portfolio. This also would see much lower returns in the long term. Typically the average price move for UK short-term bonds is 1.9%

So take all the above-mentioned ideas and find the balance that is right for you. Do you **need** the money within 5 years or 25 years?

I Still Don't Have a Scooby

If you're still wanting to invest into the stock market but are unsure about the approach you want to take, then I suggest using the following chart to help you create a plan, or you could seek financial advice.

On the next page, you will see a tree created by PensionCraft (this can be found on YouTube or https://pensioncraft.com/). This is known as the 'Scooby Doo' chart. PensionCrafts charts help to visualise an investing strategy, Scooby Doo being wild (high risk) but fun and Velma being boring (low risk) but relaxed. It is split into 3 sections: international bonds, national bonds (or vice versa if you are not resident in the UK) and equities.

A simple 'safer' strategy would be to choose an investment that interests you from each section and balance how much you invest into each. As you can see, PensionCraft has chosen a USD government bond, a UK corporate bond and the Volatility factor. This shows that they are perhaps betting on interest rates to increase (we will cover interest rates later).

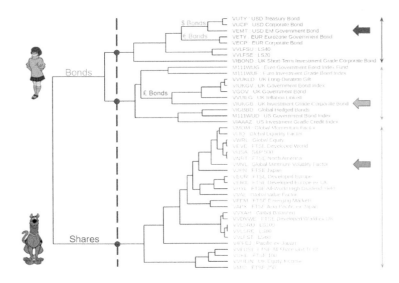

*Also, before I move onto the next risk, bear in mind that funds that are close together on the chart also move together, so it is advised to invest into separate branches.

Politics

Although it may seem obvious to some, it might not be to others; politics has a huge and consistent impact on equities for good/for bad. A current example would be the ongoing trade war between the US and China, causing global upsets with import/export laws being enforced.

However, this can be seen as both good and bad for investors, depending on where your money is resided. The 'war' is causing a shortage in certain required materials, for example, the current shortage is semiconductors; this has a massive effect on tech companies that do not have access to national semiconductor suppliers. On the opposite page, American semiconductor producers have now got the upper hand as everybody is turning to those companies to create contracts, benefiting the US market in the long term.

Whenever there is political unease, you tend to see equities fall and commodities/bonds rise temporarily; when the sanctions ease, the table turns. This is why it is important to take this into account and have investments that do well during times of uncertainty and the opposite.

Interest Rates

Although interest rates aren't consistently impacting the market, they do appear to have an effect on the market every now and then. For example, if the Bank of England announces that they are to increase interest rates, this shows that either inflation is expected to rise or the economy is growing too quickly. Rises like this prompt retail banks to also increase their interest rates, making bonds fall in price, which in other words makes bonds more attractive to investors, subsequently creating equity sell-offs to purchase bonds.

Inflation Risk

Inflation happens year over year within economies all around the world. This is something that can't be prevented completely, although central banks can try everything in their power to lessen the rate of inflation. Inflation does not tend to directly affect the market as long as it is a slow, gradual, natural increase.

However, if your investments are not keeping in line with the rise in inflation, then over time, you are losing money on your investment. This is most relevant when looking at bonds, as they do not always yield big enough returns to keep alongside inflation. In terms of equity investments, companies can adjust their prices to reflect inflation, meaning that your equity stock should naturally keep up with inflation. The same applies with real estate.

Inflation-linked bonds, i.e., Vanguard's UK inflation-linked gilt, is a good way to hedge yourself against inflation.

Credit Risk

Although fairly uncommon, it is best to not eliminate credit risk. This is where a company or governmental body cannot repay the creditors (bond holders). Luckily for investors, bonds are attached to a 'credit rating' that is split into various classes, AAA being the highest and most secure credit rating.

You can see the full list of classes on Wikipedia under the 'Bond credit rating' article.

Currency Risk

Last but not least is the risk to investments when currencies change values; when the GBP rises, foreign assets will be less valuable and vice versa. This is known as 'FX impact'.

Although hard to predict as a beginner investor, if you are clued-up when it comes to the economy, there is the ability available to everybody to be able to invest in GBP based bonds/equities if the investor believes that the GBP will perform strongly in years to come.

There is also an option to invest in GBP-hedged foreign assets, for example, the iShares $USD Treasury Bond, which essentially uses GBP to fund the bond whilst exposing it to USD.

(STOCK MARKET)

Once you familiarise yourself with the risks of investing, managing your stock market portfolio correctly is the next step in order to achieve your investing goals. There are multiple layers when it comes to managing an investment portfolio. I won't be going into depth about this. I suggest researching online, buying a course or a book, or speaking to a financial advisor.

However, I will briefly outline the various indices to managing a portfolio.

Starting with **margin of safety**, argued to be the most valuable principle in investing, margin of safety is the process in which an investor only purchases an equity when the equity market price is below their value. Margin of safety works alongside value estimations. Before purchasing an asset, investors typically use multiple calculations to work out the value of an investment (we will talk about this later on in the stocks/shares section) through fundamental and technical analysis. Once a valuation has been made, the investor will then look to buy at a price below the intrinsic value (with the exception of extremely solid enterprises that allow for compound investing).

Importantly not only for your willpower but also for an accurate valuation, an investor will tend to **invest in assets in an industry that they understand**. If you understand the economics and the future of an industry, then it will work better for you. If the stock starts to underperform short term, you should not be panicking because you have chosen something that you know is going to succeed in 5-10 years' time. Instead, the price declining is an opportunity to acquire more, to bring down the average cost and to raise your returns when the stock eventually rises.

Another principle that disciplined seasoned investors prioritise is **measuring the company's performance rather than the company's stock price**. Just like it says on the tin, you need to be measuring their performance because the stock price simply follows what the company's performance is visualising. If they're performing poorly in comparison to competitors, then their stock price is going to follow a downside trend, but if they are performing well, then guess what? Their stock price is going to rise upwards alongside their performance.

DO NOT invest in a stock solely on **speculation** and trends in social media. Do your research into the company, make sure they have the fundamentals, make sure they are not already overvalued, make sure that you like the product that they are delivering, check their competitors, and find out if they are already being out-performed.

Minimize the cost, minimize your expenses and minimize the fees. Fees, commissions, taxes and ask-bid spreads are found in all corners of trading and investing. An investor will want to keep these to an absolute minimum, because after a long duration of time (we're talking 10-50 years), these fees certainly do add up. Here's an example:

"Imagine that you are 21 years old in the 1960s. You plan to retire on your 65th birthday, giving you 44 financially productive years. Each year, you invest $10,000 for your future in small-capitalization stocks. Over that time, you would have earned a 12% rate of return. If you spent 2% on costs, you would end up with $6.5 million. It's certainly not chump change by anyone's standards. Had you controlled frictional expenses, keeping most of that 2% in your portfolio compounding for your family, you'd have ended up with over $12 million by retirement, nearly twice as much capital." - Joshua Kennon (thebalance.com)

All in all, an investor wants to be keeping eyes open at all times for up-and-coming opportunities. They want to be keeping costs low whilst maximising potential. Every decision that an investor makes should be based upon fundamentals, statistics and research as opposed to speculation and online articles.

Which Sector Do You Prefer?

Investing should not be a boring, mundane chore, and it certainly does not have to be stock-market oriented. Investing should be something that excites you. This is why it is important for you to kickstart your financial future by seeking which sector you **want** to invest into.

(REAL ESTATE)

Some investors prefer to invest into real estate because they like to get hands-on and physically be able to see their assets grow. Property investors also enjoy the thrill of researching areas that are up-and-coming to try and catch a bargain property before the market inflates in that particular area.

However, investing into real estate does not just involve buying a property and then selling it. There are multiple different ways in which an individual can invest and get their money into the property market. Let's take a look at the different ways.

1. **Rental Property**

   If you invest into **rental properties,** you will become a landlord; this means dealing with people and clients. Will you be comfortable in this position? Can you handle responsibilities such as paying the mortgage, taxes and insurance, maintaining the property, finding new tenants and dealing with any raised issues from current tenants?

If not, do not worry. If you're still wanting to invest into rental properties, but do not want to face any issues or angry tenants, luckily for us there are lovely property managers who will take care of the issues for you. Usually a property manager will take a cut from your monthly rental income of around 10%-15%.

One way that you will make money through property is by collecting rent. Typically, you are in control of how much rent your property will cost per month, depending on factors such as location, size and utilities. A strategy that you want to try and achieve when renting out property is to cover your expenses until the mortgage is paid off, which is when rent becomes profit.

If you want to stop gaining passive income from the property and liquidate it, you are essentially raking in pure profits as the rental tenants have paid your mortgage for you whilst your housing has increased in value over the many years you have held it.

Here is another mundane graph, this time showing UK housing prices from 2007 to 2020:

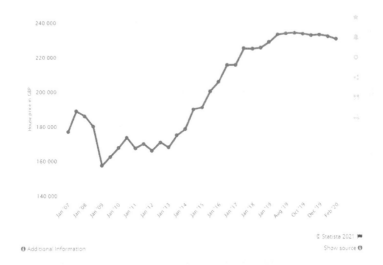

As you can see from the graph above, UK housing prices have drastically increased since 2007, going up to around £230,000 from just below £180,000. With the current ongoing pandemic, you may be able to find some "cheap" house bargains to begin your real estate investing extravaganza.

2. **Flipping Real Estate**

House flipping is when a real estate investor buys houses and then sells them for a profit (or potentially a loss). In order for a house to be considered a flip, it must be bought with the intention of quickly reselling. The time between the purchase and the sale often ranges from a couple months to a year.

Real estate flipping is a completely different pathway compared to the laid-back, long-term approach from rental properties. Flipping properties is a very hands-on experience. To get maximum profit from doing so, you will more than likely need to learn how to DIY. We all know how much labour costs!

House flipping is also a **very high-risk** approach to investing. It solely seeks those short-term returns, which can end up either being a dream or a disaster.

A successful flip can be achieved in multiple ways:

- You can buy a property that is marked up cheap because it is rundown and in dire need of repairs and tender loving care. Once repairs have been carried out and the property is up to standards, the flipper will then sell for a hopeful profit. This is why you want to keep labour and material costs as low as possible, even if it means getting your own hands dirty.

- You can buy a property in an area that is rapidly rising in popularity and house prices or maybe an area that is getting infrastructure upgrades such as broadband, bus/train stations, schools, jobs, etc. Without carrying out any expensive repairs, they will resell at a higher price.

A few tips for flipping houses and maximising profits:

- As mentioned earlier, learn how to DIY! Take courses in useful construction trades to learn how to build a home from top to bottom by yourself. Media platforms such as YouTube are also amazing resources in the modern world to learn the basics.

- Use cash not loans! Don't add debt into your balance sheet by taking out loans to pay for properties. Using cash means that you do not have to rush to sell your property, as you do not have to worry about paying back the loan/increasing interest rates.

- Research the area. What price do houses typically sell for in this area? Does the area have the necessities to make houses sell quickly to eager buyers? Can your property give you a big enough profit margin from a renovation in comparison to nearby houses of the same size?

- Ask a real estate agent for advice. Estate agents in the area will be able to point you in the correct direction of a "nice" neighbourhood for your budget and price target.

- Research material costs for the necessary work and try to create a budget before you buy the property.

Do not forget about the current circumstance of your nation. Right now there are many risks when it comes to all aspects of investing. **Brexit** has proven uncertainty in the property market, so make sure to do your research on how our independence could affect the property market in the short term.

Do not forget that **coronavirus** is also making changes to the economy worldwide. Not as many people have got the capital to buy property right now, and others are waiting for stabilisation in the markets before making their purchases.

3. **<u>Real Estate Investment Trusts (REITs)</u>**

If you are wanting to invest into real estate but do not currently have the capital for all the glamour of actually buying properties, then do not worry. These options are easy and affordable ways for investors to get their hands on the real estate market.

What is a REIT? A real estate investment trust is a company that invests at least 75% of its assets into different types of property. These companies can be invested into by using a stock exchange. If you were to search 'REIT' into any stock broker database, you would be met with hundreds of different names.

There are two different **major** types of REITs:

- **Equity REIT**

An equity real estate investment trust is the most common type. These trusts will generate income through rental spaces such as offices, retail stores, shopping centres, apartments etc. The trusts will then pay a large amount of their income out among shareholders via dividends (if you want to find out what a dividend is, check the Stock Market section).

- **Mortgage REIT**

A mortgage based trust does not own real estate; instead, they fund projects and earn their income via the interest generated on these investments.

However, if you do not want to invest into a single real estate investment company, you can also invest into an **ETF (exchange-traded fund),** which is a way for you to invest your money into a wide spread on the property market rather than an individual company.

An example of a real estate ETF is **iShares UK Property UCITS ETF.**

4. <u>Crowdfunding Property</u>

Last but not least, another beneficial way to invest into property without needing a large starting capital is property crowdfunding.

What is property crowdfunding? This is a type of real estate investment where multiple or many investors pool together their fundings to buy a property or property development. Typically they will either contribute small or large percentages of the total amount depending on what the investor can afford. This is a fast way to raise money for the investment.

Once the crowdfund has purchased the investment, returns will be shared between the individuals. For an equity investment, the rental income will be shared as well as any capital appreciation generated by the underlying value of the property. For property development or property loan investments, the returns will be generated via interest on the lent funds.

An example of how property crowdfunding works. You want to invest into a property in a certain area because you believe property prices in said area will rise in the next few years. However, you do not have the capital to outright purchase a property, so instead you combine what you can currently afford to invest, alongside other individual investors who are in the same boat.

To do this you would typically use a property crowdfunding platform (can be found anywhere on the internet with the correct research) and contribute your pot of money to the total amount, for example, £1000 of your money to purchase a £150,000 property that has a net dividend yield of 3.5% (annual income from rent after fees etc. have been counted for).

Once you have contributed your funds, you now own your share of the property. The returns depend on how much you have contributed to the pool. The more you contribute, the more you return, just like a stock.

A Few Personal Tips For Buying Real Estate

Just like any other investment, it is a wise idea to have a set of personal rules or budgeting schemes to help protect you from the risks of investing.

Here are a few of my tips when it comes to buying property:

- **Maximise the deposit on your mortgage.** The higher % you pay up front, the better loans you find. Increase in increments of 5% to see changes. The **ideal target for a deposit on a mortgage is 20%.**

- **Have 3 times your property's monthly expenses saved up** in case of damages, loss of tenants, and loss of other income. This will be your parachute if any emergencies happen.

- **Hire a property manager** to help relieve the stresses of dealing with tenants and property issues.

- **Work out the true cost of buying**: mortgage fees, legal fees, valuation fees, stamp duty tax, surveys, removal costs, repairs, furnishings.

- Make sure to start this journey with a fantastic **credit rating** to prevent any rejections on loans and to maximise your bank's trust. There are plenty of apps/websites that are free to use that enable you to track your credit rating.

(BASIC COMMODITIES AND RARE GOODS)

Very popular amongst investors, particularly for diversifying portfolios and maximising returns, are commodities. Commodities are basic goods that are considered investments.

As the demand becomes higher for the goods, the cost increases. Of course this also means that if the supply increases and the demand decreases, the prices will lower.

Commodities are the oldest form of investments. Think about the Egyptians with their jewellery, spices and silk in the Middle East/Asia, and sugar and tobacco in the West.

Basic goods date way back before any kind of real estate/ stock exchange. They are a consistent recurrence in human history.

Not only can you physically see, secure and show off your investments, but they tend to hedge investors **against the effects of inflation**. Demand for goods tends to be **higher during times of high inflation,** pushing up the cost of your investments.

However, **commodities are not immune to risks.** They can be extremely volatile, mostly more volatile than other forms of investments. Be especially wise about this before investing into futures (a contract with an expiration date following predetermined prices), as you are not able to back out whenever you need to. I suggest staying away from futures/ leverages/margins until you are extremely confident with the market.

Before you rush to your nearest supermarket to stock up on cucumbers, let us have a look at current types of basic commodities and rare goods that may interest you.

(CRUDE OIL)

Crude oil is an extremely important commodity. It is also a basic necessity (currently) that is becoming scarce on our planet. If you have an interest in investing into crude oil, it is best that we understand what affects the cost and how you can invest in oil.

After crude oil is extracted and produced, it gets refined into many everyday products. Examples include fertilizer, makeup/cosmetics, ink, plastics, pharmaceuticals, synthetic fibre and many more than we realise.

Petroleum being the product that creates the most demand in almost every country in the world whether it's to fuel cars, lorries, motorbikes, helicopters, airplanes, ships or ferries. Petroleum is widely used across every automotive/aerospace/marine sector.

Crude oil generally reacts to these levels of demand; more demand + lower the supply = higher the prices. When demand lowers, the supply can be easily matched, resulting in lower prices. A recent example would be during the pandemic lockdown, you may have noticed car fuel prices were much lower than normal as a result of less people using the roads.

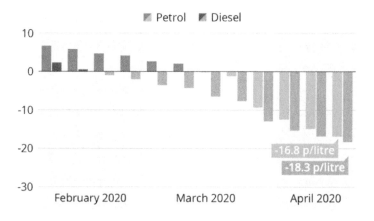

Sources: Department for Business, Energy & Industrial Strategy

This graph taken from statista.com shows fuel prices within the UK in 2020 compared to the prices in 2019. As you can see in February 2020, the prices were higher than those of February 2019, but you will then notice as less people were driving due to lockdown enforcements across the UK in March 2020, the prices took a sudden plummet towards the end of April 2020.

Geopolitics vs Crude Oil

As an investor in crude oil, it is extremely useful to keep track of geopolitics (political risk as spoken about earlier in the Risk Management section) because geopolitics has a giant impact on the crude oil sector.

As economies such as China/India grow, the demand for oil is ever increasing. As war breaks out, the supplies decrease, i.e., Middle Eastern tensions. The Middle East is important to us as this is where most of the world's oil is produced. Another example of a geopolitical circumstance that caused crude oil prices to drastically change would be the 2020 Russia - Saudi Arabia oil price war, when these two countries battled to have lower oil prices, causing the cost of oil to fall 34% in the US.

How to Invest in Crude Oil

Unfortunately, crude oil is unlike the other commodities. It is not a physical asset that you can hold and show-off. To invest into oil, you will need to consider either purchasing stocks in oil companies, crude oil ETFs or crude oil mutual funds. These methods can all be found on the stock exchange.

Crude oil does not need to be invested into directly; you may also want to consider investing into energy sector funds that also invest in crude oil companies. This will also help you to diversify your portfolio and lower your risks.

(GOLD AND METALS)

Finally, we can show off our investment! All jokes aside, gold is a loved investment by many investors. This is because it has proven growth over the years. Although gold is not the only metal that is heavily invested in, other metal commodities also include silver, palladium, platinum and copper (lithium is also upcoming).

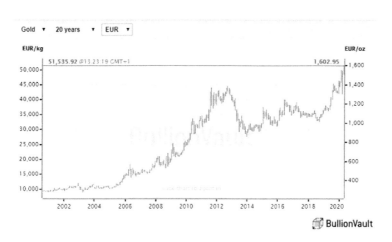

This graph by BullionVault shows the growth in the price (EUR) of gold per kg/oz from 2002-2020.

Why Invest in Metal?

During periods of uncertainty and volatility, you often see investors turn to these precious metals due to their status of reliability. Investors also hold onto precious metals to hedge their portfolios against high inflation rates and currency devaluation, once again managing our exposure to risks.

Like crude oil, metals follow the strict rule that an increase in demand will increase the prices. Think about all the places that metals are used… there are MANY! From technology in your phone to the structure of your house, metal is used almost everywhere and is being stripped from the planet every single day.

Base metals such as aluminium and copper are widely used in all levels of construction and industrial applications. They are inexpensive because they are commonly found all around the world; demand can be easily matched by supply.

Because of their wide usage across industries and their ever-growing global demand, the prices are forever being positively impacted.

How to Invest in Gold and Metals

Unlike crude oil, you can physically hold gold. To do this, an investor may purchase bars, coins and even objects such as watches/necklaces/statues. I personally recommend using a legitimate bullion website to purchase your gold and storing it somewhere such as a safety deposit box at a bank or a vault.

However, if you're not interested or not fussed about holding your gold in a physical form, just like oil you can also invest into stocks, ETFs and mutual funds. Whether it's a physical gold ETF, shares in a mining company, a production company or an exploration company, make sure to do your research (due diligence) into the company or ETF beforehand to make sure it is the right choice for you and to discover what the company's risks are.

On the contrary, you may not want to physically hold onto the cheaper metals such as silver, aluminium and copper. Because of their cheaper prices, investors would need a much bigger supply in order to see profitable returns. Instead you can either invest into base metals companies or ETFs.

(WHISKY AND WINE)

If you're an alcohol lover, this might become your new favourite sector of investing, but please understand that this requires research, bartering and the willpower to not open your bottles. As consumers' favourite whiskies and wines become rarer, they are willing to pay that little extra in order to relive the taste of their favourite alcohol.

> ➤ This graph by rarewhisky101.com shows the 'Rare Whisky 100 Index' which includes 100 iconic collectors' bottles of whisky from 2012-2021. As you can see, the price has drastically increased (+273.20%).

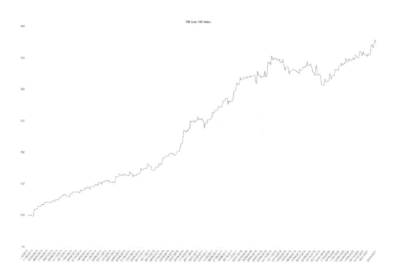

Please understand that these are expensive bottles of rare whisky, a bottle of Jack Daniels' will not have the same growth as a 60-year-old bottle of Macallan.

You will need to research whiskies and wines. What has demand? What has a small supply? Is the factory where it was produced closed? Is it aged? What type is it? Can you afford to buy it?

Typically whiskies and wines are a very long-term investment unless you can get your hands on an extremely rare whisky at an auction or cellar. Also keep an eye out for limited editions; plenty of alcohol companies love to release limited edition

bottles. If it's a 1 of 300 release, then you can expect your bottle to become valuable very quickly. If 200 are drunk by consumers, then your bottle is now 1 of 100.

When storing whisky or wine, please be very mindful about the conditions. If they are in direct sunlight, more will evaporate through the cork or the taste may go off. If you store them in a cask, eventually it will evaporate through the oak. Ensure they are stored upright so the cork is not facing unnecessary pressure. Keep the temperature lower than room temperature to reduce evaporation (hence why cellars are typically used), but be mindful of cellar humidity. Be sure to use a dehumidifier so that the wood and labels are not damaged. Is it a screw top bottle? Make sure the cap is retightened every now and then.

The Commodity Conclusion

Investing in commodities is definitely recommended. It is a great way to diversify your portfolio therefore helping to reduce your portfolio's weaknesses. The above are of course not the only materials that you can invest into. In fact, almost all hobbies have items that you can invest into; famous collectibles are being sold daily across the world.

Whether it is paintings, autographs, cars, celebrity items, Pokémon cards or stamps, there is a collectible for everybody so if you have something that interests you it may be worth buying and holding a limited item that could be seen as a nostalgic collectible in the future!

(CRYPTOCURRENCY)

Cryptocurrency or 'crypto' is:

- Decentralized - not controlled by a government or central bank.

- Global - used worldwide (no need to worry about exchange rates).

- Digital - stored in digital wallets rather than leather ones.

- Currency - just like today's cash, it will hopefully be used for regular transactions.

Investors are currently ploughing into cryptocurrencies as they are a hybrid of an investment and also a commodity. Not only is crypto seen as a protection against a failing economy, but it is also a potentially highly profitable investment.

Please however do not think that it is completely safe; crypto is still exposed to risks. It is still completely new, which means that we do not have the long-term data or valid statistics for a period of time to show how different global circumstances cause different reactions in the market.

The asset is also continuously seeing high volatility due to the sheer volume of trading, meaning if it goes up quickly, it can also come down as quickly. There are multiple factors causing the volatility:

- People buy in hopes to get rich quickly, but when the coin value goes down, they panic and sell their coins, leading to a chain of sell-offs.
- Speculation in the media (whether good or bad).
- Less liquidity in comparison to regular financial markets.

However, as we see cryptocurrency grow and become popular, there are signs that the volatility is starting to stabilise; whether or not it will ever follow volatility patterns in regular assets is yet to be concluded.

A Few Facts

- Most crypto payments cannot be refunded/ reversed, so be careful who you send it to.

- Crypto coins are a little like emails; nobody controls them other than the user.

- Today there are over 4000 cryptocurrencies in contrast to 2013 when there were only a few.

DO YOUR RESEARCH beyond the basics. You need to understand what it is that you are investing into. If you believe in your investments and understand that they have potential, the negative comments should not bother you, and trust me, there will be a lot of negative comments about everything you invest into. I strongly recommend learning about the origins of Bitcoin and Blockchain, understanding where they originated and how they grew.

HOW TO INVEST MONEY (PT. 2)

Educate Yourself

Investing your money does not always have to be about seeing numerical returns; investing into your **education** is equally as important, if not more important than investing  into money generating assets. It is also permanent. Everybody has something that they have thought about learning, so take action, invest into a course and learn! If you are of more intellectual value to companies, you will eventually be paid accordingly.

Whether it is a course in marketing, financing, computer coding or painting, out there somewhere will be a company or individual willing to pay you more depending on how skilled you are.

More education means **more earnings**, meaning the **more you can invest,** which also means the more potential you have to **start your own business**.

Money is not always a necessity for investing into education. There are plenty of free articles and videos online to educate yourself within the market you are wanting to invest into, because when it comes to investing those hard-earned pennies, an investor wants to feel confident that they are not gambling away their money. The best way for you to feel confident in your investments is to research into the field, into the company, into the property and the area. Will it have demand in the future? What's the competition? Is the buying price overvalued?

This is known as **<u>due diligence</u>** (we will cover this in-depth later).

Emotions

No matter who you are, sometimes emotions do get the better of us. However, when it comes to investing our cash, it is important to change your outlook on money. "IT IS ONLY A MEANINGLESS NUMBER WHICH HAS THE ABILITY TO REJUVENATE" were the exact words that I kept telling myself whenever I saw an investment down by

30% or more, and believe it or not, seeing numbers in the red does not even slightly phase me anymore.

No, this is not because I've gone clinically insane, but this is because I've put my personal time and effort into researching the investments beforehand. Therefore, I know that the company has strong fundamentals and a very credible future. If you believe in the future of your investments, then you have nothing to worry about in the short term. Money is just a tool and sometimes tools can break, but that does not stop us from our objective. Sometimes to see victories you have to take defeats.

Panicking when an investment temporarily slides can cause emotions to take control of the situation, which most of the time **causes more harm than good**. If an investor sells an investment at its lowest, they are either minimising their returns or taking a loss, and then once the stock starts to rebound, they become fearful that they will miss out so they buy back into the stock, maybe this time even more expensive than they had sold it for. This is a terrible loss and more often than not becomes a vicious cycle. This is a great example of why your mindset is key to your success.

> "Be fearful when others are greedy and greedy when others are fearful."
> — Warren Buffett.

Investing vs Saving

Referring back to the very first chapter in this book, we discussed why saving money is not necessarily the best pathway to growing wealth. I'd like to take this opportunity to give an example comparing investing vs savings. It is important to bear in mind that this is hypothetical.

If a person were to begin at the age of 21 years old with a job earning £30,000/year with an average of 3% in annual appraisals, if they had saved 15% of their annual paycheck every single year until the age of 65, that person would have saved themselves roughly £400,000 after taking away average expenses.

Now, that is not a bad sum of money. In fact, to most of us, that is A LOT... Right now. However, once you factor in inflation and possible negative interest rates (savings account), this actually won't be enough to retire with, especially if you want to live your life or upsize your house. But what happens if we invest that money rather than save that money?

If the same person were to compound that 15% income every year with a 4% annual return, by the time they reach 65, it would have become £900,000. Much better! Sounds almost affordable to live your life, but wait—we are not done yet; 4% AR is statistically quite low with the Dow Jones Industrial and Russell 2000 averaging 7% AR for the past 20 years.

So now that £900,000 becomes £1,900,000. If you are an incredible investor and 7% AR is not quite good enough for you, then why not push it to 10%? Now you are looking at £4,800,000 by the time you are 65.

Compound investments are incredible, right?

I think it's safe to say you can now enjoy all the holidays you want, treat your children, their children and still have enough piggy bank to play golf every weekend on your favourite course.

Businesses and Side Hustles

If a person has an entrepreneurial mindset, then starting a business might be the right route for them. There are plenty of ways to start a business: it may be online, it may be franchised, it may be run out of their home. Business sounds like a scary word to most, but on the contrary, it can be exciting, especially when you turn one of your favourite hobbies into a steady flow of income.

A few examples of hobbies would be writing (like me, right now), photography, dancing and singing. Although it may not be a first thought, all these can become a way to make money. You can start a YouTube channel, create an outsourcing company, or perform freelance jobs (sites such as Fiverr are great).

There are plenty of ways to make extra money on the side, but before you begin, expect yourself to spend a lot of time, money and effort on marketing to be able to start generating the income flow you desire. The more you invest into a business, the more it will eventually return. Just do not give up or shy away from temporary losses if it is truly what you want!

HOW TO UNDERSTAND TAXES

Taxes are an important part of our lives and the economy. This is something we all wished we were taught in school. In fact I'm sure at some point in your life you would have said, "They should teach people about taxes in school".

DISCLAIMER: These tax figures will be relevant to the UK as of 04/2021. If you reside in an international country or are a time traveller, you may want to research appropriately.

Income Tax

In the UK, there are multiple streams of taxes that an individual will be exposed to. Income tax is usually the first of these, a tax that we all discover the hard way as deductions on our paychecks.

As an employee, all income tax is automatically deducted by the employer through a system familiarly named 'PAYE' - 'pay as you earn' is a system that allows employers to easily navigate their tax deductions and send payrolls through to HMRC.

It is important for all employees to keep on top of their payrolls, ensuring that they are being paid and taxed the correct amounts. Calculating your gross pay (income before deductions) is simple: multiply your hourly rate by your hours worked for the month. If you are on a fixed salary, this should be the same each and every month unless you have been given a bonus or an appraisal.

Once the employee has ensured their gross pay is correct, the next step is to verify that they are being taxed correctly. Tax years (fiscal years) run from 6th April to 5th April the following year; each and every tax year allows an employee to earn up to a certain amount before being taxed on their income. The year 2021/2022 accommodates a £12,570 tax-free personal allowance. Personal allowances need to be kept in mind when working out your tax amounts. However, if an individual earns over £100,000 per annum, they may have a reduced personal allowance (depending on circumstance).

Income Tax Rates:

0% up to £12,570 per year

20% for £12,571 - £50,270/year

40% for £50,271 - £150,000/year

45% for earners over £150,000 per year.

Example

If an individual was to earn £55,000 a year, their annual tax would look like this:

0% on the first £12,570

20% on the next £37,700 = -£7,540

40% on the next £4,730 = -£1,892

Resulting in a £9,432 income tax deduction for the year, leaving the employee with £45,568. To work out the monthly income tax deduction, divide your annual deduction by 12 (months). In this example, the individual would be taxed £782 each month. Although, this is not the only deduction.

National Insurance Contributions

NI is a privilege to pay since these contributions pay for all our benefits when we are in need: state pension, NHS, jobseekers allowances, maternity allowances and also other support allowances. There are three separate classes: Class 1 - Employees, Class 2 - Self Employed, Class 3 - Volunteers.

As a Class 1 – Employee, you begin to pay NI once you earn more than £184 per week. Once again, this is paid in percentages: 12% of your earnings above £184 per week up to £968/week; if over £968 per week, the deduction rate falls to 2%.

Example

If an employee earns £2000 per week, their NI deductions will look like the following:

0% on the first £184 per week.
12% on the next £967/week = -£116.04/week
2% on the next £849/week = -£16.98/week

Totalling in a NI contribution of £532.08 per month equalling £6,384.96 contributions per year.

REMEMBER: Gross Pay - before deductions. **Net Pay** - After deductions (the full amount received).

TAX CODES

When an employee begins work, they must supply a P45 from their previous employer. P45s show the new employer how much tax the employee has paid so far in the fiscal year. An individual starting their first ever job will have to fill out a new starter checklist. Both of these forms will guide the employer to decide which tax code best suits the new employee, so be sure to double check your forms and ensure that they are error-free.

What is a 'tax code'?

A tax code is a crucial piece of information for employers and HMRC. The four-digit and one-letter codes help to decide how much an employee is to be taxed. These codes show how much a person can earn before being taxed, circumstantially varying depending on how much the individual earns, how much tax they have already paid in the year and their current personal tax allowance.

For this tax year, the typical code will be '1257' and a letter, i.e., 1257L, which translates to £12,570 before taxation. Other examples include:

- ## BR

If your tax code **starts with BR,** you are not getting a tax-free personal allowance. Instead, you will be liable to pay a 20% basic rate on all income. This can happen if an employer does not have the correct info to work out the appropriate tax code. This can also be seen if you are working two separate jobs and instead HMRC allocate the personal allowance to one job rather than both.

- ## K

If your tax code **begins with K,** this could mean you have previous taxes that need to be paid, or you receive income or job perks that cannot be taxed, for example, a company car.

- ## Emergency Tax Code

An emergency tax code is given when your tax code does not match current circumstances. This tax code will not take into account any reductions that you may be entitled to; you will pay more tax than expected. However, this will be refunded by HMRC once corrected. Emergency tax codes will appear as: 1257 W1, 1257 M1, 1257 X.

Be sure to check your pay slips and make certain that your taxes and tax codes match your circumstances. If you believe that anything is incorrect, you should contact HMRC as soon as possible and correct it or find out why.

Capital Gains Tax (CGT)

Capital gains tax is an important tax to understand for every investor. If you are liable to pay CGT, then you must do so correctly. Although, there are a multitude of ways you can reduce your CGT per year. Capital gains are taxed from 'realised' profit, meaning the profit that you have made **after** deduction of your initial investment. The most common investments that are susceptible to these taxes are stocks, corporate bonds, metals and real estate (this does not include your family home).

Just like income tax, in the UK, we have a tax-free allowance of £12,300 on capital gains, meaning you will have to profit over £12,301 to begin paying CGT. What is important to remember is that any **losses** that you make deducts itself from your realised profits. This is a lot to remember when trying to calculate how much you owe HMRC, as well as the calculations you also need to be making note of; details of buy-and-sale prices, dates when bought/sold and any other details such as fees or tax reliefs.

Capital Gains Is Paid On:

- Personal possessions worth £6000+ (excluding personal car)
- Investment properties
- Stocks and shares (non-ISA)
- Cryptocurrency
- Any inherited assets when sold

Capital Gains Is Not Paid On:

- ISAs/PEPs
- UK gov gilts and bonds
- Betting and lotteries

How To Reduce Your Annual CGT

Firstly, if CGT is owed, it must be reported to HMRC; **taxes must be paid.** On the contrary, there are multiple ways to reduce your annual bill. Making use of the annual tax-free allowance of £12,300 is foremost, as this cannot be carried over to future years. If two people are married, they can push this to £24,600 due to the allowance being per individual. If an investor has a part of their allowance left over at the end of the tax-year, it may be wise to use it all up by selling an asset for the desired amount followed by re-buying the asset. Keep in mind that in tax rules, you must **wait 30 days** before rebuying multi-asset funds. If losses were made in abundance and total more than the realised profits, this can be reported to HMRC and carried over into future allowances.

Making use of an ISA is another tool that can reduce the amount of tax paid. ISAs have a deposit limit of £20,000 per year and are not exposed to taxation. ISAs will be discussed within the next chapter.

HOW TO OPEN AN ISA

A n ISA, or individual savings account, is **only available to those who reside in the United Kingdom.** They are simply accounts that help people save or invest money with multiple benefits. ISAs were first introduced in 1999 and are exempt from taxation upon returns (this is because the money going into the account would have already been income taxed), so this is a great way to make returns on your money tax-free! You can only have one ISA of each type open at a time, and you **must** stay within the £20,000 limit across them to avoid being taxed.

Since 2017, there are four types of ISA:

Cash

These types of ISA are quite simple. They really are just a cash savings account. However, you will earn tax-free interest on your savings within the cash ISA. In most cases, these cash ISAs will offer higher interest rates than your bank account. It is absolutely worth opening one to use as your savings account if you are not interested in the alternative options.

Cash ISAs have an overall contributions limit of £20,000 per tax year (for year 2021/22). You will not be able to deposit more than this amount into your account. If you withdraw money from this account, it will not reset your annual limit unless you are using a flexible ISA.

You can only open one cash ISA per year, but it is possible to transfer to another cash ISA or a stocks & shares ISA during the tax year. If you want to change providers, you must ask your new provider to carry out the transfer in order to keep any savings free from tax.

Flexible ISAs open you up to flexible facilities such as being able to withdraw and replace the money within your ISA without reducing your annual allowance. Not all will allow this, so please check the small print that is provided!

Be Aware (Cash)

- Some providers lure you in with jaw-dropping interest rates to begin before stooping to a low interest rate. Make sure you do your research and prevent this from happening. Although, if this does happen to you, look for a higher rate ISA to transfer your savings into.

- Check the small print to see if there is an early withdrawal penalty. You do not want to be paying a penalty if you cannot afford to do so. Another way to avoid this is to not deposit money that you cannot afford to let go.

- Fixed-term cash ISAs that are offer very high interest rates usually follow the performance of an index or commodity price. This means that there are usually a set of rules that need to be ticked before you start to see capital growth, for example, the S&P 500 increasing by 7% over a certain period. This can be seen as a gamble.

Cash - Help to Buy Scheme

I will keep this one short and sweet, as the UK government closed this type of ISA in 2019. Hopefully, they will reopen it within the near future. This scheme was to help first-time buyers afford a home by providing a 25% bonus on top of their savings (up to £3000).

Stocks and Shares ISA

As somebody who invests into the stock market, this is my absolute favourite type of ISA. It allows you to deposit up to £20,000 per tax year into the account, and the returns made within that account are CGT exempt (up to a certain limit)! Tax-efficient, just how we like it.

Once again, please be aware that there are risks with investing, so definitely consider the other risk-free ISAs before you dive deep into S&S ISA. Investments are always a medium- to long-term commitment, so if you want to withdraw your money in the next few years, I recommend using an alternative ISA.

Stocks & shares ISAs are vulnerable to fees; these are usually based on the broker in which you are investing with, so have a snoop around and ensure you are checking the small print for fees.

Innovative Finance ISA

An innovative finance ISA, also known as P2P lending, is a form of investing in which you lend money to borrowers, whether individuals or businesses. Once they have borrowed your money, they will pay back the amount with the added interest on top. The interest gained is your return made (tax-free). If you are a basic tax payer, you can earn £1000 in interest tax-free; a higher tax payer can earn £500.

These can be rewarding as some providers offer great interest returns. However, there are risks to be factored into the equation:

- Defaulting - in which the borrowers could default on their repayments.

- Slow cash withdrawal time - you may have to wait to be able to access your own money.

- Not protected - IFISA are not protected under the Financial Services Compensation Scheme, meaning your money could be at risk if the IFISA provider goes bust.

- Contingency Fund - IFISA providers have a reserve to protect your money against defaulting, but this may not protect you if multiple borrowers default at the same given time.

As with all ISAs, make sure you read the print. How long will your money be tied up for? What are the returns looking like? What is the minimum deposit? How much are they charging in fees, i.e., management fees?

Lifetime ISA

Unfortunately, this type only applies to those within the 18–40 bracket. The lifetime ISA is used to buy your first home or save money for later life. You are able to put in up to £4000 each year until you are 50 years old (you must make your first payment into your ISA before you are 40 years old); the government will then add a 25% bonus to your savings up to a maximum of £1000 per year.

You are able to hold cash or stocks and shares within your lifetime ISA (or a combination of both). Once you turn 50, you will no longer be able to make payments into the ISA or receive the bonus, although you will still earn interest on your cash or returns on your investments. **You can only withdraw if** buying a first home, aged 60+ or terminally ill.

HOW TO BUILD YOUR CREDIT SCORE

I f you have never heard of a credit score or credit rating, do not worry, you will still have one (implying you have used some sort of financial borrowing before) . In basic terms, it is a rating from numbers 300 to 850 that banks and other financial lenders use to judge whether or not you are worthy of borrowing from them. To check what your credit score is, you will need to find a credit referencing agency. I advise using one of the main three if you are from the UK - TransUnion, Equifax and Experian.

Your score will keep track of credit accounts that you have held and whether or not you have kept up on credit repayments such as paying your phone bill, overdrafts, credit card, car finance, and mortgage payments on time. This also applies to joint accounts. Credit scores do not reflect the balances of your bank accounts, your spending habits or salary; they simply monitor your borrowing and repayments.

The higher your credit score, the better. If you have maxed-out your credit rating, this will make you incredibly attractive to financial lenders and greatly increase the chances of you being able to borrow the amount that you need and even in some circumstances interest-free. Each different credit reference agency scores people slightly differently, as they use alternative calculations and different ranges of numbers. For example, Experian uses 0–999, a good score being 881–960, an excellent score 961+ and an average score between 721 and 880. Whereas Equifax uses the scores 0–700, a good score being 420–465, an excellent score 466+ and an average score 380–419.

How To Improve Your Credit Score

Have you checked your credit score? Is it on the low end? Not to worry.

You will have a bad credit score if you have failed to make repayments in a timely fashion. Credit defaults will stay on your credit history for six years whether or not you have paid off the debt. After all, how can somebody lending you money trust you if you have a history of not paying back? Bankruptcies, IVAs and CCJs also poorly affect your credit score once again taking six years to be removed from your credit history.

So how do we improve? Firstly, if you are struggling with debt, please seek guidance. Contact your lender and be honest with them. It is so much better for you to speak to them and tell them that you are struggling as opposed to repeatedly missing your payments. Here is a little checklist to help you improve your score:

- Pay above the minimum when making repayments. Paying the bare minimum makes lenders presume you are scraping together pennies to be able to afford to pay back.

- Register on the full electoral register. This will help companies find out who you are. If they cannot, then it will be harder to get credit.

- Pay your bills on time, every time. Pay for insurance upfront as opposed to monthly.

- If you rent, look into the rental exchange initiative, a way to turn rent payments into good credit.

- Use a credit card for SMALL but OFTEN spending only, such as filling up on petrol or weekly shopping. This shows lenders you are capable of managing their money wisely. Not having a credit card can actually reduce your credit score. Try to spend under 30% of your credit card limit. Credit building credit cards exist too (very high interest rates, be sure to pay off monthly) for those who cannot apply to a regular credit card.

HOW TO BUY YOUR FIRST HOME

Buying your first home is definitely a daunting task, for absolutely everybody and anybody. However, as long as you are clued-up, have done your research and do not dive in head-first unaware of the complexities, you should find it an unchallenging, exciting and joyful task to overcome. Let's take a look at first-time-buyer mortgages.

What Is A Mortgage?

Starting with the bare basics of buying a house is understanding what a mortgage is and how they work. A mortgage is a loan that is provided by a bank or a building society that enables you to buy a property. However, you will not entirely own the property until you have completely paid off the mortgage; you will only own the percentage you have paid for.

Once you have gotten yourself a shiny new mortgage, you will then pay back the amount you borrowed from the lender plus the interest that they charge on top of that over a certain period (usually around 25 years). If you fail to repay your mortgage, the lender is obliged to repossess your home.

It is likely that you have heard of a mortgage deposit before; this is a down payment paying for a part of the property up front. If the property costs £400,000 and you are making a 20% deposit, you will need to pay £80,000 upfront. The lender will then pay for the other remaining £320,000, which you will then owe over the duration of the loan; this is known as LTV or loan-to-value.

95% Mortgage Guarantee Scheme

As you may or may not be aware, on 1st April 2021, the UK government launched a scheme to 'guarantee' 95% mortgages, meaning buyers are able to access 5% deposits on mortgages. This was launched to encourage banks to start lending again after withdrawing during the pandemic.

As tempting as a 5% deposit mortgage sounds, I personally would not recommend this. In most cases, the lower the deposit, the higher the interest rates. It is best to save up to a more comfortable spot before putting down a deposit; 20–25% deposits are preferable to minimise interest rates.

However, 10–15% is a very common down payment due to affordability.

Help to Buy Equity Loan

Another alternative to paying a tiny deposit is the 'help to buy' equity loan; this is a loan from the government that will cover 15–40% of the property price, depending on where you live; up to 40% in London and up to 20% in the rest of England and Wales, meaning you will have to put down a deposit of at least 5% and get a mortgage to cover the rest. Keep in mind that this type of loan is **only applicable to new-builds**.

This has its benefits: you will only need a 5% deposit and you are only taking out a 55–75% mortgage, giving you access to better mortgage rates. These loans are for a percentage of the property value rather than a fixed amount, meaning you could end up paying back more/less depending on the value of your home when you sell. Let's take a look at an example: You have been given a 20% equity loan to buy a new build property worth £400,000; this will be a loan of £80,000. You then want to sell the same property in the near future valued at £420,000; you will now have to repay £84,000 - 20% of the new value. Of course if the property fell in price, you would repay less.

Right to Buy Scheme

If you are a council tenant, this may be amazing news to you. The right to buy scheme is a UK government scheme that allows tenants to get up to £84,200 off the cost of buying their council house (up to £112,300 in London) - figures may not be accurate as this changes alongside inflation.

To be eligible for this scheme, you will need to have been a tenant for at least 3 years under a landlord who operates for the council, NHS trust or housing association. Further rules apply. The property needs to be your only home and self-contained, you cannot be declared bankrupt or have an undischarged bankruptcy, you cannot owe money to creditors and you must have a secure tenancy.

Guarantor Mortgages

If you cannot afford to buy a property through a traditional mortgage, a guarantor mortgage is an alternative option, giving you the chance to get accepted or to borrow more. However, you will need a family member or a very good friend willing to be at hand to make repayments if you cannot afford to do so. They also need to be a homeowner and be willing to risk losing their own home if you are unable to keep up with repayments.

Some guarantor mortgages are available with a 0% deposit, meaning the mortgage covers the entire price of your home (also meaning that you do not own any percentage until you make payments). Once again, just like the 5% deposit scheme, I do not recommend going below 10% on your deposit due to high interest fees.

Remember

Your credit score affects how much lenders are attracted to you. If your credit score is low, you will struggle to find mortgage providers. There are mortgage calculators online that will help you find out how much you are able to borrow; this can be useful even if you are not looking to buy a home just yet.

There are other factors to consider before buying your first home, so make sure you do your research before you fully commit to such a big deal. I have only highlighted various types of mortgages to support first-time buyers; there are many other layers to buying a home.

HOW TO SEEK FINANCIAL ADVICE

Firstly on a personal level, I want to thank you for taking your time to read this. It means a lot to me knowing that I may have potentially supported or inspired someone to get out of a dark place financially. Financial anxiety causes a lot of stress and turmoil in households, so it is incredibly important to be clued-up and to never get yourself into money trouble.

However, as stated before, I am not a financial advisor, and this book is just about my opinion and approaches that I have personally taken to get myself financially stable over the past years.

It is very important that you seek advice from a professional when you are not sure what to do with your money or what decisions you need to make about your financial future.

Financial advisers can help with:

- Retirement plans

- Investments

- Savings

- Making the most out of a big sum of money

- Buying property/mortgage guidance

- Being flexible around big financial life changes, children/divorces

Make sure that your financial advisor is qualified and registered. They must have a Level 4 or above in the relevant field and an SPS certificate updated annually. They must be registered with the FCA. If they are not, make sure you report them to the FCA.

Before you look for the right financial advisor, you need to know what your financial goals are. Are you planning to afford your children's future? Are you planning to buy a new home? How much risk are you willing to take (we spoke about risk previously)? Short term/long term? Do you want investment advice? Are you looking for advice or information? Do you want a one-off advisory session or an on-going relationship with your advisor?

I wish you all the best and hope that you never have to struggle financially. If you are struggling, I hope that you reach out and find the correct support that you need.

Printed in Great Britain
by Amazon

24570288R00059